THE USBORNE BOOK OF
PAPER
FLOWERS

Ray Gibson

Edited by Cheryl Evans • Designed by Ian McNee
Illustrated by Prue Greener • Photographs by Amanda Heywood

First published in 1994. Usborne Publishing Ltd., Usborne House, 83-85 Saffron Hill, London EC1N 8RT. England.
Copyright © 1994 Usborne Publishing Ltd.
Printed in Portugal
UE. First published in America March 1995.

Paper and techniques

This book shows you how to make all sorts of flowers out of paper. Some are very easy and some need a bit more skill. They are not all exact copies of real flowers and they are not all just for putting in vases. The pictures on the right show some of the things you will find useful. A list at the start of each project tells you exactly what you need each time. Below are some of the basic techniques you will use.

Paints and paintbrushes, thin cardboard, old newspapers.

Single crepe paper (or double crepe, from craft suppliers), tissue paper, wrapping paper.

Making templates

Templates are shapes you cut around to make petals and leaves for paper flowers. On pages 30-31 are all the templates you need for the flowers in this book. Here's how you use them. Lay tracing or greaseproof paper over the template. Trace the shape with a pencil. Usually, you then use it like this:

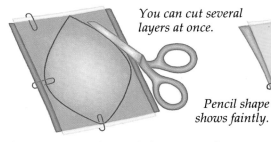

You can cut several layers at once.

Pencil shape shows faintly.

Cut a square around the shape. Paper clip it to the paper you need for a petal or leaf and cut it out. Move the paper clips around as you cut.

Sometimes you are told to copy the shape onto paper or cardboard. Turn the tracing over and go over the pencil lines. Then cut it out.

Half templates

If the shape is a half template, fold your tracing paper and align the fold with the flat side. Trace the half shape.

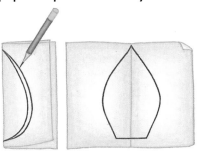

Turn the tracing paper over and draw over the lines you can see through it. Open out for the complete shape.

Binding stems

To bind wire stems, use green florists' tape or cut a narrow strip of green crepe paper, across the grain (see right). Wind the tape or crepe strip tightly around the wire from the top, slanting down.

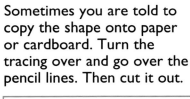

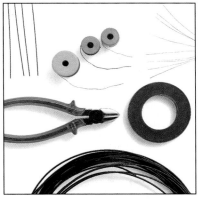

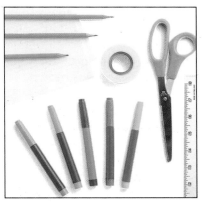

Glue stick, PVA (household) glue, sewing pins, ribbons, paper clips.

Stem wires, silver wires, green tape (all from florists'), heavy garden wire, pliers, thread.

Felt tip pens, pencils, clear tape, scissors, ruler, tracing (or greaseproof) paper.

Crepe paper grain

If you look closely at crepe paper, it has lots of little creases running along it. This is called the grain. If you ease the creases apart, the paper stretches without tearing. You can use this to make the shapes of crepe paper flowers more realistic, by cupping, fluting or stretching, as shown here.

Frilling

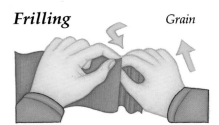

Grain

Hold the crepe up with the grain vertical. Bring your left hand closer to you, gently twisting and stretching the paper over your right thumb.

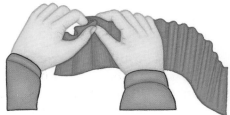

Keep moving the paper to the right a little, then bending gently in the same way again to make dents all along the edge. This gives a wavy effect.

Cupping

Grain

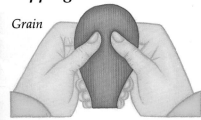

Cut out the shape with the grain going up and down it. Hold it, placing your thumbs where you want to cup.

Gently pull your thumbs apart. The wrinkles stretch out and the crepe paper becomes curved like a cup.

Stretching

Hold the edge you want to stretch with both hands and gently pull the grain apart. Move along and pull again until the whole edge is stretched.

Spring flowers

You can quickly make enough of these flowers for a small posy. They all use the same stem. See how to make it at the bottom of the page and prepare a few first.

Things you need:
Scissors, glue stick, pencil, tracing or greaseproof paper, paper clip, dressmaking pin, thin cardboard.

For daisies you also need:
3 squares of white tissue paper 9 x 9cm (4 x 4in), yellow tissue paper 20 x 12cm (8 x 5in).

For daffodils you also need:
Yellow crepe paper 15 x 12cm (6 x 5in).

For quick twist flowers you need:
2 contrasting sheets of tissue paper 17 x 17cm (7 x 7in), scrap of yellow or orange tissue paper, saucer, thread.

Make several flowers, wrap in tissue paper and tie with a bow for a posy like this.

Bend the straws gently to arrange the flowers.

Straw stem

You need:
Green tissue paper, 20 x 3cm (8 x 1½in), straw that bends.

Glue one long edge of green tissue paper. Roll the straw up in it, starting from the unglued edge.

Daisy

1. Put the squares of white tissue together. Trace and cut out the daisy shape on page 30. Draw around it on the top tissue square.

2. Mark the middle dot through all layers with a pin. Take off the tracing, paper clip the layers of tissue together and cut out.

3. Bend, but don't crease, the petals in half. Make a 1cm (½in) snip with scissors at the pin hole. Bend the other way and repeat.

Don't press along the folds.

Daffodil

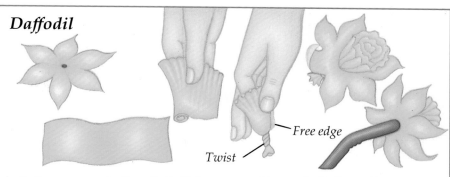

Free edge

Twist

1. Follow steps 1- 3 of the daisy, using one layer of yellow crepe. Cut a yellow crepe strip 5 x 12cm (2 x 5in).

2. Frill (see page 3) one long edge. Wind the frilled edge around the tip of your first finger. Twist the other end tightly.

3. Pull it off your finger. Glue down the free edge. Stick the twist through the petals. Glue into the stem.

Quick twist

Do not crease the folds.

1. Place a saucer on your two sheets of tissue. Draw around it, then cut out the circles. Cut both layers at once.

2. Bend the circles in half across, then in half again, sideways. Twist the corner and tie with thread. Gently pull the petals apart.

3. Make a ball of the yellow or orange tissue paper, dab it with glue and press into the flower. Glue twist into stem.

Tap on a hard surface.

Tail

4. Crumple up the 12cm (5in) square of yellow tissue paper. Flatten a little and put it on the 7cm (3in) yellow square.

5. Bring up the sides of the yellow square and twist. Tap to flatten it again. Poke the tail through the snips in the petals.

6. Lick your fingers and gently twist the layers to fan them out around the middle. Glue the tail and stick it into the stem.

Pop-up flowers

Things you need:

Stiff, bright paper 40 x 18cm (16 x 7in), flowers cut from magazines or wrapping paper, bright wrapping paper 8 x 4cm (3½ x 2in), florists' silver wire (or use fuse wire), white paper, glue stick, scissors, clear tape, pencil, ruler, tracing paper, felt-tips, paper clips.

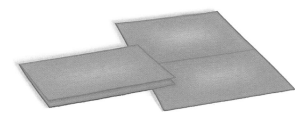

1. Cut a piece of the bright, stiff paper, 28 x 18cm (11 x 7in) for your card. Fold the short sides together and press the crease well. Open out again.

You can make cards of different shapes and sizes. Change the sizes of pieces A and B, too.

This card is decorated with small anemones, like those on pages 24-25.

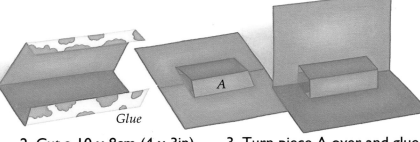

Glue

2. Cut a 10 x 8cm (4 x 3in) piece of the same paper (A). Fold the short sides to meet. Fold over 1cm (½in) at each short end and glue all over.

3. Turn piece A over and glue it flat onto the middle of the card, matching up the creases. When it is dry, close the card and press the crease.

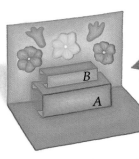

4. Cut another piece of stiff paper (B), 6cm (2½in) square and repeat step 2 with it. Open the card, match the crease in B to the top edge of A and press.

5. Take the bright wrapping paper 8 x 4cm (3½ x 2in) big. Glue it onto the lower half of piece A. Glue cut-out flowers onto the card above piece B.

Glue on a bowl shape at step 5, if you like.

If you can find an envelope to fit your card, glue flowers onto it, too.

6

Only glue the part that sticks to piece B.

6. Glue a cluster of cut-out flowers as wide as your card onto white paper. When dry, cut them out. Glue them to the lower half of B.

7. Make another flower cluster on white paper to stick onto the top of the lower part of piece A. Check what it looks like before you glue.

8. Trace the butterfly on page 30 Cut it out roughly. Paper clip onto folded white paper. Align the body with the folded edge.

9. Cut around the traced shape through both layers of white paper. Decorate the wings with felt-tip patterns.

10. Tape a short piece of silver wire or fuse wire along the crease with clear tape. Tape the free end under the top part of strip A.

11. Bend the wire so the butterfly hovers over the flowers and does not stick out when you close the card. Add flowers to the front of the card.

Write a message in your card, if you like.

7

Crocus bowl

For the bowl you need:

A bowl 13-15cm (5-6in) across and 6-9cm (2½-3½in) deep, kitchen foil, PVA (household) glue, a soft cloth, blue and white tissue paper, 1 or 2 sorts of thin, patterned wrapping paper, thin cardboard, craft knife, 7 used matchsticks or cocktail sticks, garden wire, black paint, paintbrush, dry tea leaves.

For 7 crocuses you need:

21 sheets of 5 x 7cm (2 x 3in) purple tissue paper, 7 pieces of green crepe paper 6 x 10cm (2½ x 4in), tracing paper, scissors, glue stick, 40cm (16in) heavy garden wire, pliers, green florists' tape (or green crepe strip - see stem binding, page 2) yellow powder paint or turmeric (a yellow spice powder), paper clips.

1. Turn the bowl upside down and smooth kitchen foil over it. Smooth and press the folds flat with a soft cloth.

2. Cover the foil with PVA glue. Tear scraps of blue tissue paper roughly 4cm (1½in) square. Stick them on all over, overlapping.

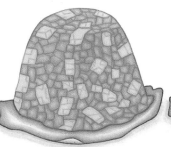

3. Cover the blue tissue with glue. Add another layer of blue, glue, then a layer of white tissue squares. Cover it all with glue.

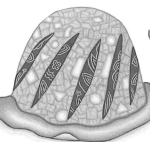

4. Tear shapes of patterned paper and glue them on. Overlap with some foil shapes, too. Leave to dry for a day.

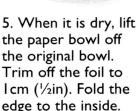

5. When it is dry, lift the paper bowl off the original bowl. Trim off the foil to 1cm (½in). Fold the edge to the inside.

Cut here.

6. Place the original bowl upside down on the cardboard and draw around it. Cut the circle out ½cm (¼in) inside the line.

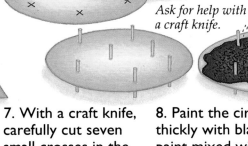
Ask for help with a craft knife.

Shake off excess leaves.

7. With a craft knife, carefully cut seven small crosses in the cardboard. Poke a matchstick through each to mark it.

8. Paint the circle thickly with black paint mixed with PVA glue. While it is still wet, sprinkle dry tea leaves all over it.

9. When it is dry, pick it up by two of the matchsticks and place it carefully to fit inside the top of the bowl you have made.

Crocuses

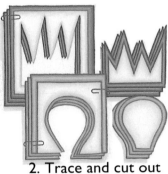
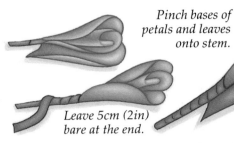

Pinch bases of petals and leaves onto stem.

Leave to dry.

Leave 5cm (2in) bare at the end.

1. For each crocus, cut 14cm (5½in) of wire with pliers. Paint the top 2½cm (1in) with PVA glue and roll in the yellow powder.

2. Trace and cut out the templates on page 31. Paper clip petal to three sheets of purple tissue and leaves to green crepe. Cut out.

3. Glue the bases of three petals and wrap around the yellow end, overlapping. Bind the stem (page 3) with green tape or crepe.

4. Wrap the leaves around the bases of the petals and glue the end down. Put a crocus stem in place of each matchstick.

Gently pull the leaves away from the petals to get a natural look.

Trim the stems with pliers if the bowl is too shallow and crocuses fall over.

9

Red roses

What you need:

I sheet red, I sheet green crepe paper, florists' stem wire 30cm (12in) long, 3 silver wires, thread, glue stick, tracing paper, 2 paper clips, pencil, scissors, ruler.

The petals

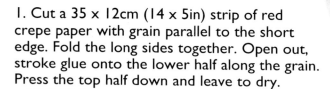

1. Cut a 35 x 12cm (14 x 5in) strip of red crepe paper with grain parallel to the short edge. Fold the long sides together. Open out, stroke glue onto the lower half along the grain. Press the top half down and leave to dry.

Hold with paper clips.

Don't cut here.

2. Trace the rose petal template on page 30. Cut out the whole frame shape.

3. Have the red crepe strip, fold nearest you. Bend the short sides together three times.

4. Put the flat base of the petal shape along the edge nearest you. Cut it out neatly.

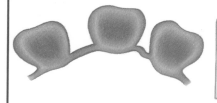

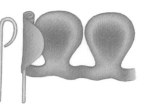

Flat edge

5. Open out the petals and cup the middle of each one (see page 3). Don't stretch the base strip.

6. Bend one end of the stem wire down by 2cm (1in). Roll the first two petals tightly around the loop.

7. Carry on less tightly, overlapping petals. Pleat the base onto the stem as you go. Tie with thread.

8. Trace the sepals on page 30. Cut them out of green crepe. Glue the flat edge and wind it around the petals.

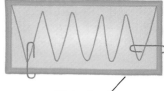

The leaves

Fold paper to cut several leaves at once.

For this bouquet, make slightly bigger roses, with longer stems. Wrap them up in cellophane.

1. Trace and cut out the rose leaf template on page 30. Cut it out six times from green crepe. Spread glue on three leaves.

2. Place a fine silver wire along each one. Press another leaf on top. When they are dry, put their wires together and twist.

The stem

Slant down.

Pull gently.

1. Cut a long strip of green crepe 1½cm (¾in) wide. Glue one end, wrap it around the base of the rose, then down the wire.

Fan out the leaves.

You could buy some white gypsophila flowers (fresh or dried) to put with them.

Add a big, red bow and a heart-shaped red label.

2. About 4cm (2in) down the stem, lay the silver wires of the leaves alongside the stem and bind them in as you wrap.

11

Sunflower

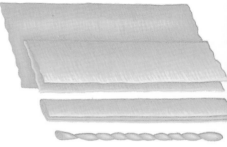

Things you need:
Round, plastic lid (from a margarine tub, for instance), brown poster paint, paintbrush, scissors, green and yellow crepe paper, any wrapping paper, PVA (household) glue, glue stick, double-sided adhesive tabs, tracing paper, pencil, paper clips.

1. Mix brown poster paint with a little PVA glue. Paint roughly around the edges of the top of the lid, and down the sides. Leave it to dry.

2. Cut three strips of yellow crepe, 30 x 10cm (12 x 4in) big. Fold the long sides together twice and crease. Twist each into a tight rope.

Press ends of ropes down firmly.

Brown paint shades the ridges and creases.

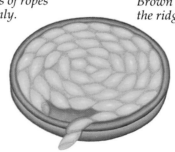

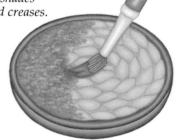

3. Paint the top of the lid with PVA glue. Wind the end of one rope around on itself into a flat spiral. Press this onto the middle of the lid.

4. Keep winding the rope around itself and pressing it onto the lid. Where it ends, start with another rope, until the lid is full.

5. Dip a paintbrush in the brown paint. Wipe it on some newspaper until almost dry. Brush it all over your spiral then leave it to dry.

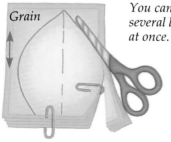

You can cut several layers at once.

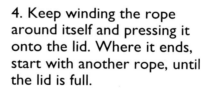

Don't overlap petals.

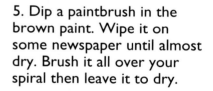

6. Trace the petal template on page 31. Cut it out and paper clip it to a piece of yellow crepe, 16 x 10cm (6½ x 4in) big. Cut out 16 petals.

7. Turn the lid face-down and spread 3cm (1½in) glue stick around the edge. Cup (page 3) the widest part of a petal. Fold a pleat in the flat edge.

8. Turn the petal over and stick to the glued edge of the lid. Do the same with more petals and glue them all around the lid side by side.

12

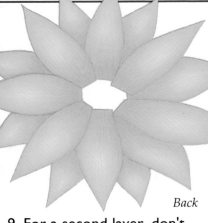

Back

9. For a second layer, don't stretch or pleat the petals. Glue stick the bottom edge, then stick on in between the others. They will overlap.

10. Fold and twist a long rope of green crepe 25cm (10in) wide, as in step 2. Stick it with tabs onto a window. Make it curve. Stick the flower head on top with tabs.

Put the pot next to the window sill.

11. Trace the leaf template on page 31. Cut three green crepe leaves. Cut a wrapping paper flower pot shape. Stick it over the end of the stem.

Stick leaves on alternate sides.

Découpage boxes

Découpage (say, day-coop-aaj) means "cutting out". You cut out flowers to decorate these boxes, then varnish them with glue so they shine.

What you need:
A light, wooden box, such as for cigars or camembert cheese, PVA (household) glue, glue stick, water-based paint, fine sandpaper, big paintbrush, flowery wrapping paper, old newspapers, ruler, scissors.

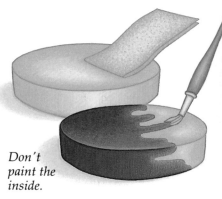

Don't paint the inside.

1. You can use any shape box. It may have a separate lid or one with a hinge. Carefully remove any labels.

2. Rub the outside lightly with sandpaper. Mix paint and a little PVA glue. Paint the outside of the lid and base.

3. Leave the box to dry. Apply a layer of PVA glue all over the painted surfaces. Leave it to dry again.

4. Carefully cut a good selection of individual flowers out of the wrapping paper with sharp scissors.

5. Try out different designs with them on the box. Only glue stick the flowers on when you are happy.

Inside the box

The glue dries clear.

1. When your flower design is dry, cover the painted parts and flowers with PVA glue. When dry, do another coat.

2. Measure how deep the box is. If the lid has sides, like this round box, see how deep they are, too.

3. Draw and cut a long strip of flowery paper, as wide as the depth of the box. Glue stick it on. Repeat for the lid.

Use a strong, dark shade on the box to make the flowers stand out better.

You could cut flowers out of magazines.

You could cut out flowers you have painted yourself, such as the anemones on pages 24-25.

4. On flowery paper, draw around the lid and base in pencil. (For a flat, hinged lid, draw around the base twice.)

5. Cut out the shapes just inside the drawn line. Try them for size to make sure they fit. Trim if necessary.

6. Glue stick the wrong side of the paper and smooth the shapes into place. Leave to dry, then use to store things.

Poppies

What you need:
Red, orange, yellow, green and black crepe paper, 25cm (10in) heavy-duty garden wire, scissors, pencil, tracing paper, saucer, glue stick, strong thread, black woollen yarn, cotton wool balls (US cotton balls), tall, empty bottle (wine or soft drink), 2 freezer bag twist-ties.

Special poppies

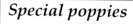

You can adapt this poppy to make very special flowers. Buy dried poppy heads to use as flower middles. Break off the real stems near the top. Loop 25cm (10in) of garden wire around just below the poppy head and tie tightly with thread to make a new wire stem. Lightly spray the crepe paper with gold paint at step 1. Let it dry, then cut out and make the petals (steps 2-4). Add a fringed middle in red crepe (steps 7-8). Attach the petals around the base of the poppy head (step 9). Bind the stem and add leaves as described opposite.

16

Petals and middle

Crepe paper fades if you leave it in bright sunlight.

Grain parallel to long edge.

Wire flat at top.

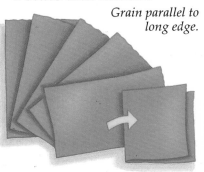

1. One flower has six petals. For each petal, cut a piece of bright crepe 25 x 14cm (10 x 5½in) big. Fold the short sides together.

2. Trace and cut out the petal template on page 31. Paper clip it to the crepe with the straight base on the folded edge. Cut out.

3. Bend one end of the wire down 2cm (1in). Bend again 2cm (1in) further down to make a triangle. Stand it in the empty bottle.

Draw around a saucer.

Tap the padded head to flatten.

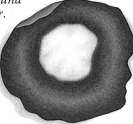

Leaves

Trace and cut out the template on page 31. Cut two sheets of green crepe paper 11 x 6cm (4 x 2½in) big. Paper clip the template to both sheets and cut out. Glue all over one leaf. Lay a twist-tie along it. Place the second leaf on top. Leave to dry. Bind the stem (see page 2). Bind in the leaf about 7cm (3in) down.

4. Cut out a circle of black crepe. Slightly cup the middle (see page 3). Pull a cotton wool ball into a disc. Glue onto the crepe.

5. Put the padded part of the crepe circle on top of the wire triangle. Pull down the edges and tie tightly with thread.

6. Cut four pieces of black yarn, 10cm (4in) long. Glue them criss-cross over the black crepe flower middle, like this.

Grain

Gather petal bases around stem.

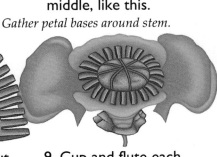

7. Cut a piece of black crepe, 26 x 14cm (10 x 5in). Fold long sides together. Stretch, then snip the folded edge finely.

8. Wrap the uncut edges of the paper around and around the flower head. Wind thread around the base and tie tightly.

9. Cup and flute each petal (see page 3). Tie two petals on opposite sides of the head. Add the rest alternately to fill the spaces.

Water lily table

What you need for each lily and pad:

3 red, yellow or pink paper napkins (unopened), yellow crepe paper 5 x 35cm (2 x 14in), grain parallel to short edge; green crepe paper and thin cardboard, both 25cm (10in) square.

To go on the table:

Sheets of tissue paper in shades of blue.

Crease folds well.

1. Take a folded napkin. Fold it in half, then half again to find the middle. Unfold it, but only back to where you started.

Start with napkin square in front of you.

2. Fold the top right corner into the middle, where the creases cross. Fold the other corners in the same way.

Hold the flaps down with your finger.

3. Carefully turn the napkin over. Fold the corners into the middle again, then turn the napkin over once more.

Use orange crepe for the middles of yellow lilies.

Lily pad mat

Draw a circle in pencil around a dinner plate, onto the green crepe paper.

Spread glue stick all over the thin cardboard. Smooth the crepe circle onto it.

When dry, cut around the circle. Cut a slit with curved corners into the middle.

Cover the table in layers of blue tissue paper. Tear wavy edges where they overlap. It may work better with a white tablecloth underneath.

Cut out and glue on orange and yellow crepe paper fish shapes.

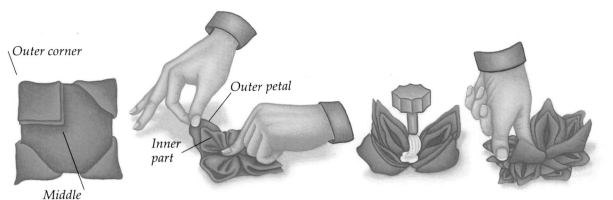

Outer corner

Outer petal

Inner part

Middle

4. Pick up a corner from the middle and pull it back over the outer corner until it lies flat. Repeat with the other three.

Scatter lilies around the table for decoration.

5. Turn over again. Press a finger on each square corner of the napkin in turn. Jerk each outer petal so the inner part lifts.

Put a lily pad at each place for a mat.

6. Follow steps 1 to 5 with two more napkins. Save the best one for on top and dab glue in the middle of one of the others.

Use a two-layered lily without a middle as a glass holder.

7. Place a second napkin on the first, diagonally, and press. Glue the best napkin on top, going the same way as the first.

Lily middle

Fold yellow crepe paper in half longways. Stretch folded edge (page 3). Fold short ends together twice.

Snip a fringe along folded edges to 1cm (½in) from open edges. Unfold strip and roll it up.

Glue loose end down. Glue the bottom into the middle of the lily. Flatten outer fronds.

19

Cactus

What you need:
newspapers, flour paste (see right), scissors, plastic tray, craft knife, thin cardboard 20 x 50cm (8 x 20in), 2 long, straight balloons, 2 long, lumpy balloons, string, plastic flower pot, green tissue paper, pink crepe paper, green paint and PVA (household) glue mixed, pebbles.

Ask an adult to help or use a balloon pump.

1. Stretch the two straight balloons with your fingers, or by filling with water. Blow them up and fasten the ends.

Flatten and spread out the petals a little.

The finished cactus stands about 1m (3ft) high.

Tape roll to balloons.

2. Tie the fastened ends together with string. Roll the cardboard around where the balloons join and tape it.

3. Cut newspaper strips about 10 x 30cm (2 x 12in). Lay lots of strips on the tray and cover with paste (see right).

4. Paste strips longways all over the balloons, from the middle out. Cover one end only with small squares of pasted newspaper.

It takes a few days to make this giant cactus but it is well worth it.

Allow a day to dry between layers.

Put pebbles on top of paper.

These are the arms.

5. Do a second layer with strips going the other way. Leave in a warm place to dry. Do three more layers in alternate directions.

6. When dry, trim the end with scissors. The balloon will go down gently. Wedge the shape into the flower pot with newspaper.

7. Blow up both lumpy balloons. Tie a long string around the end of each. Pull the string to bend the balloon and tie it around the last bump.

Flour paste

Stir 1 mug of flour and 3 mugs of water in a big saucepan.

Ask an adult to help you bring it to the boil, stirring all the time. Take it off the heat.

Allow to cool. Pour into a bowl. Cover it with plastic food wrap. Keep in a refrigerator.

Paste more strips over end of string.

Ask for help to use a craft knife.

Pinch strips into bumps.

8. Paste on three layers of newspaper. Use 10 x 10cm (4 x 4in) squares. Leave it to dry between layers. Cut off the string.

9. Cut circles in the stem to push the arms in. Make small holes first and enlarge if necessary. Paste strips over the joins.

10. Paste, then roll and twist, 15cm (6in) strips of green tissue paper. Add to the cactus in stripes. Paint green between the stripes.

In this picture, the pot is covered with sand.

Flowers

Cut a long strip of pink crepe 9cm (3½in) wide (grain parallel to short edge). Cut one long side into deep points. Wind and gather the straight edge into a roll and tie it with thread. Cut a cross with a craft knife into the top of each arm. Push the flowers into them.

21

Tiger lily and vase

What you need:

For each lily, 1 15cm (6in) and 6 12cm (5in) pipe cleaners (cut with scissors), florists' green tape, green paint, brown felt-tip pen, strong thread, tracing paper, pencil, glue stick, scissors, 12 silver wires, 46cm (18in) strong garden wire, orange and green crepe paper.

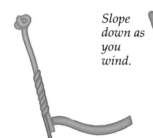

Slope down as you wind.

1. Paint the 15cm pipe cleaner green. Bind it to the top of the garden wire with green tape. Bend the top into a knot shape.

2. For a stamen, bind a 12cm (5in) pipe cleaner with green tape. Leave the top 3cm (1½in) bare.

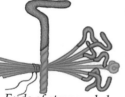

Ends of stamens below knot.

3. Paint the top brown. When dry, bend it as shown. Make five more, then bind them around the stem with silver wire.

Grain

4. Trace the petal on page 30. Cut out twelve of them in orange crepe. You can cut several at once, if you like.

Trim edges if they don't match.

5. Glue one petal, lay silver wire down its middle, then glue another on top. Do this five more times, for six double petals.

6. Add small, brown markings with felt-tip pen. There should be more at the base of the petal, and fewer at the tip.

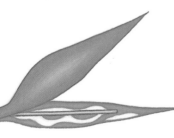

7. Trace and cut out the leaf on page 30. Cut out two leaves in green crepe. Glue them together, with a silver wire between.

Making up

1. Bind three petals around the base of the stamens with silver wire or three strands of thread.

2. Add three more petals in the gaps. Cup (see page 3) the sides of the petals down. Curl tips under.

3. Bind tape over where the petals join, and down the stem. Bind in another flower and leaves, too.

Fan out the sepals around the stem.

Arrange five lilies in the vase. Florists usually use odd numbers in an arrangement.

Vase

What you need:

A tall glass jar you can fit your hand into, large flowers cut from wrapping paper or magazines, bright scraps of paper, a damp cloth, a dry cloth, PVA (household) glue.

1. Mix the glue with a little water. Glue the paper flowers to the inside of the jar, right side against the glass. The glue dries clear.

2. Fill the spaces between the flowers with scraps of paper to make a mosaic background, the brighter, the better.

3. Wipe the outside of the jar with a damp cloth. Polish it with a dry cloth. Allow it to dry before you put your lilies in it.

Anemones

These are paper flowers you can paint yourself. Use strong, bright anemone shades for the best result.

What you need:
Strong, white paper, poster paints or inks, paintbrush, scissors, glue stick.

1. Wet a sheet of paper thoroughly. Shake off any excess. Lay it flat on a waterproof surface. Leave it for a minute.

2. Paint flowers by doing six blobs in a circle for petals. The paint will smudge and spread across the wet paper. Don't worry about this.

Gift wrap presents with plain tissue paper. Scatter flowers on the parcels with glue stick.

To make an anemone card, stick a large flower on folded cardboard, near the fold. Cut around the edge, about ½ cm (¼ in) from the shape. Don't cut through the fold in at least one place.

Choose matching wrapping paper.

3. While the paper is still wet, add a contrasting blob to each petal, a black blob in the middle and green blobs at the edges for leaves.

You can just group anemones on bright, folded cardboard to make a card.

For another kind of card, make a compact shape with flowers on your cardboard and cut around it at the top edge only.

4. Do not move the paper before the paint is dry, or it will run.

Punch a hole in one flower with a paper punch. Write on it, then tie on with ribbon.

5. Cut out the flowers roughly, then neatly, leaving a tiny white border. Cut off any extra smudging that you don't want.

25

Garland

Make this summer garland from the instructions on the next four pages. You can turn it into a Christmas garland, too. See how on pages 28-29.

What you need for the flowers:
Pink, white, yellow, blue crepe paper, strong thread, newspaper, 30cm (12in) florists' wire for each flower (you need about 25), bowl of water, red or orange food dye.

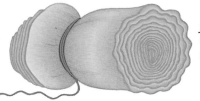

Vary the finished size of the rolls.

1. Roll up long, 5cm (2in) wide strips of crepe, tightly at first, then more loosely. Tie firmly with strong thread near one end.

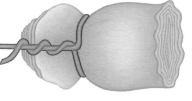

2. Wrap florists' wire around the thread. Twist the wire end around itself to hold it. Bend the wire down as a stem.

Don't let wet flowers touch.

The edges dry crinkled.

3. Dip the flower into water (with added food dye if you want to tint the edges) for 20 seconds. Lift out, shake well and stand in a jar to dry.

Find out how to make the frame and put the garland together on page 28.

Arrange big and small flowers in groups. See next page for how to put them on the frame.

Mix mottled and plain leaves. See how to attach them to the frame on the next page.

Leave a space opposite the loop to tie on your ribbon.

Leaves

What you need:
Long strips of green crepe paper, 8cm (3½in) wide (grain parallel to the short sides), dressmaking pins. You need water, green crepe and newspaper for mottled leaves.

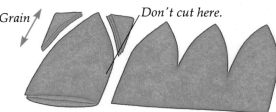

Grain

It comes out with paler spots.

1. To mottle crepe, lay it on newspaper. Sprinkle with water. Turn over onto the newspaper to dry. Cut into 8cm (3½in) strips. Use as below.

Grain

Don't cut here.

2. Fold a strip into a concertina with each fold 4cm (1½in) long. Cut curved corners off the top for a leaf shape. Open out, and cut into three-leaf sections.

3. Cup (see page 3) each leaf in one section. Pleat the base and push a dressmaking pin through the pleats to hold them. Repeat with all sections.

MAKING THIS GARLAND CONTINUES ON THE NEXT PAGE

Garland continued

To make the frame

What you need:
Wire coat hanger, newspapers, clear tape, green crepe paper, wide gift ribbon, dressmaking pins.

Don't worry if it looks lumpy.

Use the loop to hang your garland.

1. Pull and bend the coat hanger into a circle. Press the hook into a loop. You may need some help with this. Cut seven layers of newspaper into 10cm (4in) strips.

2. Fold all the strips together in half longways. Make several strips like this, then bind them all around the frame and tape down. Bind a second layer, too.

Gently pull and stretch outer layers for petals.

Flowers should stand up from the frame.

3. Wrap strips of 7cm (3in) wide green crepe paper on top. Use thinner strips for the loop. To attach a flower, wrap its wire around the frame, then around itself.

4. Arrange big and small flowers in groups. Pin leaves to the frame around the flowers. Look at the photographs here and on the last page for help and ideas.

Tie a red or patterned bow at the bottom.

Christmas garland

Follow all the steps on the last three pages, but add these extra ideas.

Tie or glue baubles among the leaves.

Paint the edges of white flowers gold.

Poinsettias are seasonal flowers.

Add gold walnuts to your groups.

What you need: Everything on page 26, plus red crepe paper, yellow tissue paper, baubles, walnuts, gold paint and brush, double-sided adhesive tabs.

Poinsettias

1. Fold a long strip of red crepe into layers about 6cm (2½in) wide. Cut one long edge into three narrow petal shapes.

2. Open the strip out and cut into eight-petal pieces. Wind the strip around and around, gathering the petals in at the base as you go.

Gold walnuts

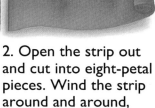

3. Flatten the petals, making them stick out on all sides. Crumple three small balls of the yellow tissue and glue them into the middle.

Paint some walnuts gold (you may have to do one side at a time). Leave to dry and stick on with double-sided adhesive tabs.

Tip

If your florists' wire is not long enough to wrap around the frame and flower, twist on another length, like this.

Templates

Here are all the templates you need for the flowers in this book. See page 2 for how to trace and cut them out: note that some are half templates and trace them as explained. The instructions for each project tell you how to use them.

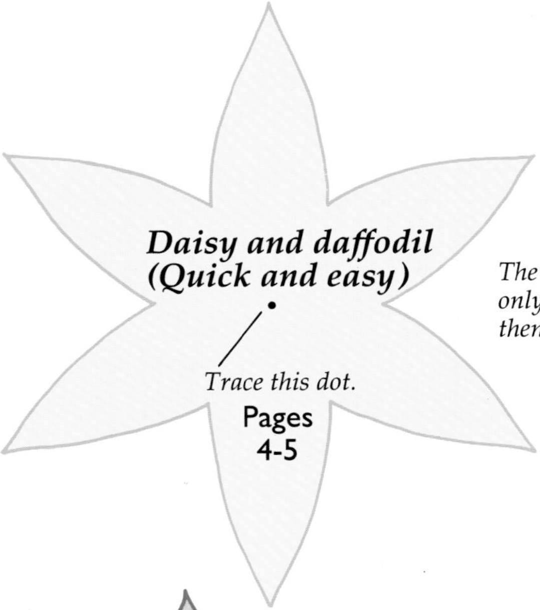

Daisy and daffodil
(Quick and easy)

Trace this dot.

Pages 4-5

Butterfly (Pop-up cards)
Pages 6-7

The butterfly is a half template. You only need to trace the half shape, then use as described on page 7.

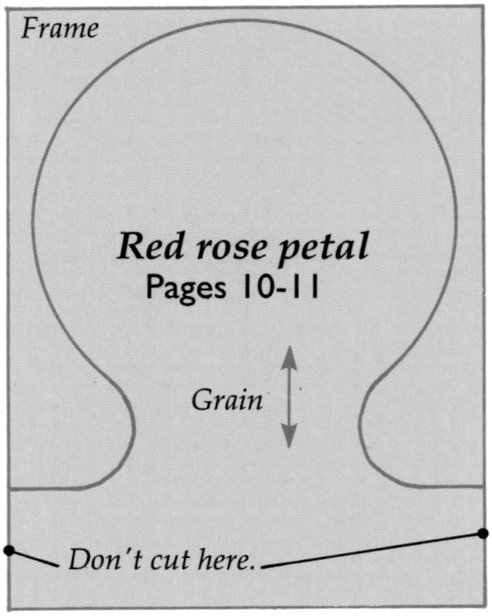

Frame

Red rose petal
Pages 10-11

Grain

Don't cut here.

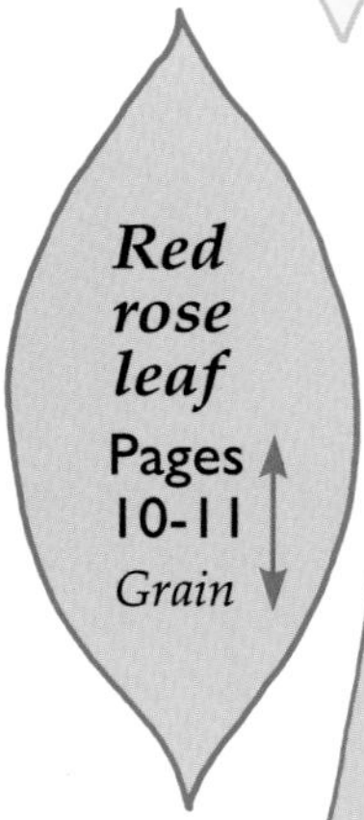

Red rose leaf
Pages 10-11

Grain

Tiger-lily leaf
Pages 22-23

Grain

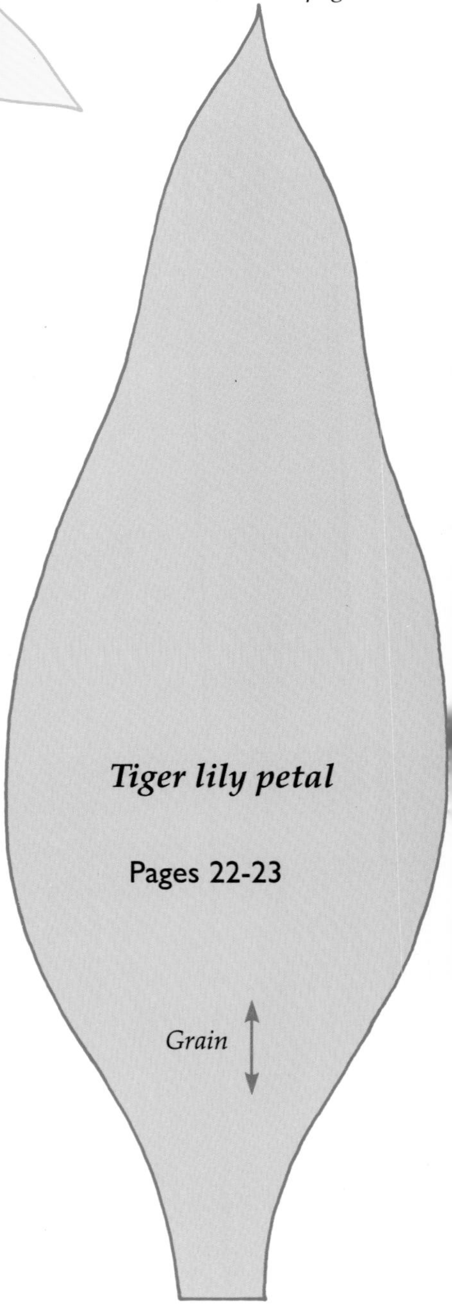

Tiger lily petal
Pages 22-23

Grain

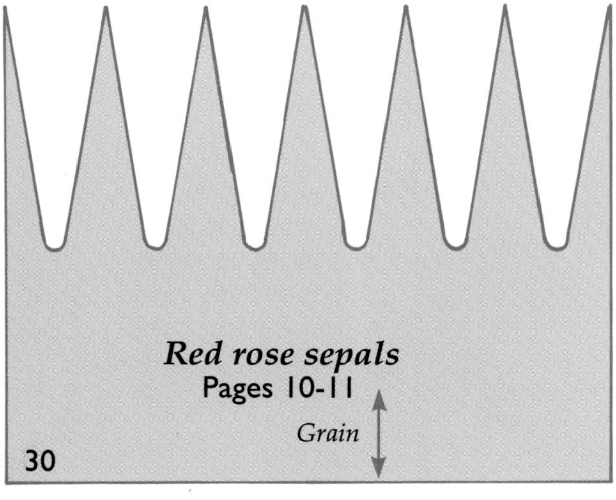

Red rose sepals
Pages 10-11

Grain

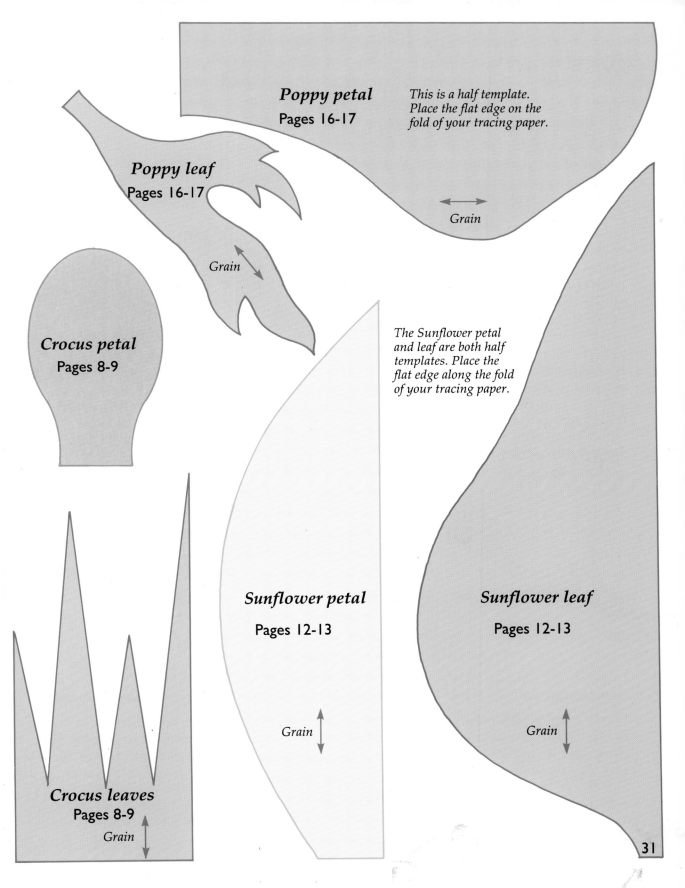

Poppy petal
Pages 16-17

This is a half template. Place the flat edge on the fold of your tracing paper.

Grain

Poppy leaf
Pages 16-17

Grain

Crocus petal
Pages 8-9

The Sunflower petal and leaf are both half templates. Place the flat edge along the fold of your tracing paper.

Sunflower petal

Pages 12-13

Grain

Sunflower leaf

Pages 12-13

Grain

Crocus leaves
Pages 8-9

Grain

31

More ideas

The pictures in this book show only some ways to display your paper flowers. Here are some more, using flowers described earlier. You can probably think of lots more for yourself.

Paper flowers make lovely presents and it is worth buying double crepe paper for something special. It is richer-looking than single crepe and holds its shape better. You can get two-tone double crepe as well for interesting effects. Specialist craft stores often stock it. Make single crepe paper firmer by spraying the flower with hairspray.

Découpage vase

Use découpage (pages 14-15) to make a vase from an empty kitchen foil roll box. Sandpaper the box, then paint with black poster paint and glue. Glue on cut-out flowers and varnish with glue.

Single rose tray

Make a single red rose (pages 10-11) to place on a crisp, white napkin on a breakfast tray. Serve it to someone in bed as a special treat for their birthday or other occasion.

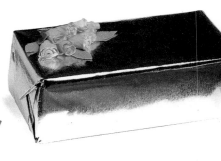

Red rose box

Cover a box from a roll of kitchen foil with wrapping paper on the outside and silver foil on the inside. Make a single red rose (pages 10-11) with a long stem to put in it as a romantic present.

Lily holders

Make a two-layered lily from napkins (see pages 18-19). Don't put a middle in it, but fill it with bath pearls for a small gift. You could even put nuts or mints in them on a party table.

Rosebud decorations

To make rosebuds, roll up and tie strips of pink crepe 5cm (2in) wide as on page 26. Arrange them and stick onto a present with glue. Cut some green crepe leaves and glue them on to cover the ends.